THE ALPHABETS OF LATIN AMERICA

Also by Abhay K.

Poetry Collections

Enigmatic Love
Fallen Leaves of Autumn
Candling the Light
Remains
The Seduction of Delhi
The Eight-eyed Lord of Kathmandu
The Prophecy of Brasilia

Edited Books

CAPITALS
100 Great Indian Poems
100 More Great Indian Poems
New Brazilian Poems
The Bloomsbury Anthology of Great Indian Poems
100 Grandes Poemas da Índia
Cien Grandes Poemas de la India
100 Grandi Poesie Indiane
Tononkalo Indianina 100 Tsara Indriandra
100 Grands Poèmes Indiens

Translated Books

Meghaduta
Ritusamhara

Memoirs

River Valley to Silicon Valley
The Colours of Soul

THE ALPHABETS OF LATIN AMERICA

A Carnival of Poems

Abhay K.

B L O O M S B U R Y
NEW DELHI • LONDON • OXFORD • NEW YORK • SYDNEY

BLOOMSBURY INDIA
Bloomsbury Publishing India Pvt Ltd
Second Floor, LSC Building No. 4, DDA Complex, Pocket C – 6 & 7,
Vasant Kunj, New Delhi 110070

BLOOMSBURY, BLOOMSBURY INDIA and the Diana logo are
trademarks of Bloomsbury Publishing Plc

First published 2020

Disclaimer: The poet's views are solely his own.

ISBN: 978-93-89867-90-9

2 4 6 8 10 9 7 5 3 1

Printed and bound in India by Replika Press Pvt Ltd

To find out more about our authors and books
visit www.bloomsbury.com and sign up for our newsletters

Praise for *The Alphabets of Latin America*

The Alphabets of Latin America is welcomingly strong. Abhay K. has a great sense of lineation, of understatement, of memorable, very particular images, and of manuscript structure. I also am moved by the way he can subtly use the elements of a place—the dream vision of Tenochtitlan (which was founded on a dream-vision) or the Borgesian paradox of looking for Borges and finding mirror reflections of the self. I love the way this abecedarian works and shifts between short and longer poems, refreshing our rhythms constantly. Also, it's such a personal pleasure for me to re see so many places that I know, through his eyes. It is a very original and thrilling book—a book that opens the borders of time and place, which is what seems so necessary now in this epoch of nationalist entrenchment and paranoia.

—**Forrest Gander**, *Winner, Pulitzer Prize for Poetry 2019*

'These snapshot poems evoking the flora, fauna, landscape and history of a turbulent continent – memories of an observant poet-diplomat organized in playful alphabetic order from anacondas to a Borges mirror, the Nazca Lines of Peru to the quetzal, samba and tango, finishing in Mexico's Plaza del Zócalo – are a glowing riot and a carnival all in themselves.'

—**Ruth Padel**, *King's College, London*

Latin Americans must be grateful, today and always, for the Indian Abhay K. and this fundamental book. Armed with intelligence and sensitivity, with calculation and passion, *The Alphabets of Latin America* is a love poem that honors us as a society and culture. In these pages, poetry, as a way of thinking and a response to adversity, reaches breadth and mastery, depth and splendor. Our region's past and present are approached not only as reading but also as experience, with the knowledge of cause and the authenticity of memory. What's more, in these texts, narrative and lyric, intellectual rigor and formal play, description and reflection happily shake hands. Likewise, identification predominates over differentiation, and an essential link is established between Indians and Latin Americans: 'A people, a tribe, a nation is destroyed, / only to reincarnate in another form.'

—**Víctor Rodríguez Núñez,** *Kenyon College, Ohio, USA*

At a time when Latin America undergoes its worst crisis in a century, Indian poet Abhay K. reminds us in his vivid verses in *The Alphabets of Latin America* of the marvels of the lands of magical realism. Widely traveled across the Americas, from Bahia to Belmopan, he has taken it all in. His poem on the Rio Carnival by itself is worth the price of the book. Without missing a beat, his lines recreate the colors, the rhythms, and the pre-Columbian roots of a region of vast, empty spaces that ache to be filled with words, as Neruda used to say. Abhay K. has done so with verve, gusto and brio, displaying a sensibility both ancient and post-modern. A riveting read!

– **Jorge Heine,** *Chile's Ambassador to India (2003-2007) & Research Professor, Boston University*

The Alphabets of Latin America is a cornucopia of delights, written by a poet who has devoted time and attention to studying, recording, and capturing experiences of place. The book is dedicated to the great poet-diplomats of the past, and Abhay K. follows in their footsteps. Many of the poems are devoted to the continent's writers, and in interrogating their stories, Abhay K. is always thoughtful and ethical; for example in his poem about Pablo Neruda, he does not shy away from more problematic aspects of his biography. What is particularly striking is that while Abhay K. does not avoid hard truths (like exploitation by colonialism), he also celebrates the joy, the vivacity, the splendour, and beauty of Latin America in this comprehensive A to Z. These are sensuous, thoughtful, playful poems, which show great devotion to a continent, its peoples, its writers, and ways of living.

— **Zoe Brigley Thompson,** *Ohio State University*

Abhay K's Latin America ranges from the haunted elegies of Neruda's Machu Picchu to the geometric precision of Niemeyer and Costa's Brasília. Latin America has gone global now, and this Indian poet's nimble and succinct alphabetical tour of it shows how essential Latin America is to world literature. The poet, 'looking at the moon from

Avenida Paulista/trying to feel the heartbeat of Latin America,' gives his own indelible perspective, yet also renders scenes in hive we can all participate.

—Nicholas Birns, *New York University*

The poem *Borges* could have been written by Borges! Abhay K.'s latest book has its fair share of realism, mixed with magic, as well as its fair share of magic, generously mixed with realism – but which is the gin and which is the tonic? One would need a Marquez to figure that one out, so just imbibe it meditatively – aphrodisiac ants and all – gratefully, unquestioningly!

—Gabriel Rosenstock, *Ireland*

Abhay K. is India's counterpart to Octavio Paz, the Mexican diplomat-writer whose poems on Indian cities, monuments, gods and culture introduced India to the Latin Americans. Abhay gives a poetic perspective of the vibrant Latin American spirit, their colorful culture, magical realism of the writers and motivates Indians with 'Oh, do not say no…Let's go to Rio'.

—R. Vishwanathan
India's Ambassador to Argentina (2007–2012)

The Alphabets of Latin America takes us on a journey through the richness and variety of Latin America with the passion and sensibility of Abhay K., a true friend of Latin Americans, in which he converses with the great poets of the region. Urban and rural, popular and erudite, traditional and modern: from Amazon to Zocalo, there are several Latin Americas depicted by the poet with a moving sensibility.

—Mauricio Santoro, *University of Rio de Janeiro*

For
Poet-diplomats Pablo Neruda, Octavio Paz, Gabriela Mistral, poetry festivals in Medellin and Nicaragua and wonders of Amazon, Machu Picchu, Atacama, Rio de Janeiro and Buenos Aires, which inspired me to visit Latin America and live and work in Brazil for three years (2016-2019) and for the warm and friendly people of Latin America

Contents

Amazon

The anaconda was missing
so they offered us piranha fishing

in consolation, and bathing
with pink dolphins in the black river

they caught the poor baby caimans
at night, while they were sleeping

and took us across the river
to meet the Indians, there were none.

Andes

The green breasts
of Earth rise
to quench the thirst
of insatiable humanity.

Atacama

i

I am here
amidst this immensity

of the cold desert,
shadows leaping out

windmills inviting
new Don Quixotes

hills rolling out and curved
supple breasts of the desert

Sun shining ever bright
in silence

not a single animal or bird,
nothing like Earth

ii

in the vastness of the desert
the road merely a line

snowcapped Andes
sibylline as ever

iii

at dawn
the moon hanging

from the sky
like a sickle

stars still bright
on the way to Lagunas Altiplánicas

iv

little hills along the Andes
like camelids' humpbacks

sunrise
lights them up in soft pink

v

an inverted pyramid
of light, air, sky, clouds

in the Laguna Miñiques
on its bleached shores

of salt
Kutz birds' nest.

Atahualpa

I, Atahualpa, the last Inca emperor,
born a sovereign, died a prisoner

mercilessly strangled by a garrote
under the cunning friar's watch

then burnt without a dignified
Inca burial, to prevent my rebirth.

Spaniards brought a strange disease
to the Andes, that killed my father

his successor died soon, plunging
the Inca empire into a succession war

Huascar and I fought for years,
subduing him, I emerged victorious

soon armed intruders entered my empire
with sixty-nine horses and a hundred more men

being ingenuous and benign, I called them
for a dialogue falling into their trap

the deceitful friar offered me a breviary
asking me to convert to Christianity

disgusted I threw it down in rage
Pizarro ordered his men to charge

a handful of them, heavily armed
butchered my army of five thousand

none of them was wounded or killed
they captured me alive in the battlefield

to be set free, I offered to fill
my cell with silver and gold

but Pizarro conducted a mock trial
and sentenced me to death by fire.

Huascar: half-brother of Atahualpa

Avenida Paulista

Avenida Paulista lures me
at night, to look at its face

I walk on its avenue stretching for a mile
flanked by countless mini Eiffel towers

boisterous young men, vivacious women
singing, relishing *rápidos*, sipping *caprioska*

couples kissing, cuddling, cooing
amor...amor... walking hand in hand

the destitute squat on the sidewalks
as installations of modern art

an empty and locked white house
glimmers at night, outside its gates

a mother sleeps holding her baby tight,
a black dog leaps over their bodies

a skateboarder rushes past them in a hurry
nearby Pele comes alive in a graffiti

making passionate love to a lady
I was warned, not to venture out

too late into the night, and yet
I'm here looking at the moon

over Avenida Paulista,trying to feel
the heartbeat of Latin America.

Rápidos: dishes which can be prepared quickly
Caprioska: a drink prepared by mixing caipirinha and vodka
Amor...amor: love...darling

Axolotl

Dear Axolotl,
the bearer of perpetual smile
the earthly rep of Xolotl
twin of Quetzalcóatl—
will someday
Latin America learn
your regeneration tricks
in full measure
and regenerate itself
healing its various wounds
or callous, ignorant
of your powers
condemn you
to extinction?

Axolotl: a native amphibian of the waterways of Mexico City known for its remarkable regeneration abilities
Xolotl: the god of the underworld in Aztec cosmogony
Quetzalcóatl: the feathered serpent

Ayahuasca

What do the indigenous tribes drink?
—Ayahuasca
What do Samba dancers drink?
—Ayahuasca

What do Latino rock stars drink?
—Ayahuasca
What do people in New York drink?
—Ayahuasca

What can cure all the ills of Latin America?
—Ayahuasca
What can harbinger a new consciousness?
—Ayahuasca

The thing is my friend
in whichever direction you turn
your ears, you'll hear—
Ayahuasca, Ayahuasca, Ayahuasca

Now the question is how to make it—
boil the ayahuasca vines over night
get up early and head to the forest
pick up lower *chacruna* leaves at sunrise

say a prayer, clean the leaves diligently
then pound it with mallet until it's fibre
brew it for several hours with water
and serve the sacred drink at the sacred hour.

Ayahuasca vines (Banisteriopsis caapi) is the main ingredient for making Ayahuasca
Chacruna (Psychotria viridis) is a perennial shrub used as a side ingredient for making Ayahuasca

Bahia

The city of all saints
    where the upper town
and the lower town
    come together
in an elevator.

Barolo Palace

On a Sunday evening in Buenos Aires
Rosa shows me divine comedy

I reach there
exactly when the tour is about to begin

she laughs like Beatriz
her voice—birdsong

we meet in hell, she accompanies me
from purgatory to paradise—

a lighthouse connecting the cities
of Buenos Aires and Montevideo across the sea

I sit in a bell jar atop the palace
pondering over the hell and heaven

Rosa makes all the difference
with her song and fragrance.

Belmopan

When the old capital was
erased by a hurricane

a new capital arose
like a condor

on a high ground
away from the Caribbean

where the river Belize
meets the Mopan

safe from the tidal waves
the Mayan civilization was reborn.

New capital of Belize was built in 1970 with its Mayan heritage in mind. Its National Assembly Building is designed to resemble a pre-Colombian Maya temple.

Bogotá

He landed in Bogotá with his eyes wide open
a little disappointed with her flatness
hoping to see her at Juana de Loca,
uneasy getting stuck
in the traffic, arriving late, making her wait
and for the first time he carried roses
across the city in his hands,
drank gin and tonic with good omen,
read poems on Dhaka and Brussels
and laughed till their stomachs ached,
said goodbye to friends, walked
to Crêpes and Waffles, ate tiramisu
and drank mint tea,
and never stopped talking all this while
thinking that night what a blessing
would it be to see each other day after day.
The next day, he looked into the mirror
and saw her face.
She appeared at Chico Park wearing
magenta trousers and a white sweater,
the day was bright, they spoke in whispers
about Borges and Marquez,
almuerzo at Canestro while it rained,
talking, digging deep into their lives
then blissful hours at the Gold museum
looking at the wonders
of the pre-Columbian world
listening to the chants of priests
conducting rituals of el dorado
offering gold to the rivers and lakes
walking through Candelaria,
in a bookstore they whispered
Twenty Poems of Love and a Song of Despair

while it kept raining, at Bendido
over gin, tonic and portobello,
they opened up as never before,
their hearts beat faster at Andido—
a mall bombed a few weeks ago,
at the hookah bar, couples danced
coming out of Chivas buses, talking
of Tinder & Happen and drugs
that made people slaves,
they said goodbyes, smiling,
feeling light, elevated, ethereal,
knowing well they'll never see each other again.

Borges

'I know of one Greek labyrinth which is a single straight line. Along that line so many philosophers have lost themselves [...].'
– Jorge Luis Borges. Death and the Compass

Looking for Borges
I came to Argentina
I found him nowhere

I searched all the libraries and cafes
all the labyrinthine streets of Buenos Aires
he was not even at La Recoleta

I found merely a mirror
and a face staring
at me in disbelief

it's hard to believe
everyone told me
Borges lived in Argentina.

Botero's Women

are
bare colossal delights
exaggerated flaunting
gentle hypnotic
inflated jumbos
Kafkaesque
lustful
mythical
nudes
out of proportion
political at times
quetzal like resplen-
-dent rotund satirical
towering urgent
voluptuous
whimsical
xeroxed
yearning
zoomorphic
but not fat.

Brasilia

'Between parallels 15 and 20,
around a lake which shall be formed;
A great civilization will thrive,
and that will be the Promised Land.'
— Don Bosco

Brasilia is mostly white
Brasilia is red laterite
Brasilia is diaphanous gossamer filled with light

Brasilia is a string of shining pearls at night
Brasilia is an exotic Turkish delight
Brasilia is a coiled serpent ready to bite

Brasilia is a village passing as a city
Brasilia is an expression in supernatural geometry
Brasilia is Italo Calvino's invisible city

Brasilia is a prophecy of Don (Bosco)
Brasilia is a poem carved in stone
Brasilia is a song of Carlos Drummond (de Andrade)

Brasilia is a diamond in the crown
Brasilia is a giant airplane on the ground
Brasilia is an Amauri village drowned

Brasilia is Clarice Lispector sleep-walking on water
Brasilia is black Acai palm dessert
Brasilia is perfection in brick and mortar

Brasilia is a piece of space cake
Brasilia is a fantasy island in the lake
Brasilia is a Dominican night shake

Brasilia is the last utopia
Brasilia is Sylvia Plath's dystopia
Brasilia is a landscape ectopia

Brasilia is an oasis of migratory birds
Brasilia is an oracle's prophetic words
Brasilia is a page from Harry Potter

Brasilia is a shifting mirage in the desert
Brasilia is a vision gone pale, blurred
Brasilia is a nail yet to be hammered.

Abhay K.

Brazilian Calabash

'*At least that's the plan.*' – Jack Turner

This fresh, green, perfect calabash I have
purchased today at the market in Brasilia
reminds me of calabashes growing
on my mother's thatched roof in Bihar

calabashes of different shapes and size.
I travel thirty years back and remember
my mother lifting me up with her hands
helping me to get to the thatched roof

to fetch calabashes to be cooked.
Now the thatched roof is gone,
replaced with corrugated steel sheets
nothing grows on it

slashed, fresh and perfect, Brazilian calabash
does not taste the same, it has too many seeds
cultivated en masse on large farms with pesticides
by some callous, half-hearted, corporate farmer.

Does anyone grow calabash
on thatched roofs these days?
I am going to cook it just like my mother
and savor it, *at least that's the plan.*

C

Caipirinha

I asked a bartender in Brasilia for a drink
she said nothing, just offered me a caipirinha

I drank it happily and asked—what is it?
She said—Brazil is body, caipirinha—its soul

Drink whiskey when in Scotland, rum in
the Caribbean, when in Brazil drink caipirinha

Curious, I asked—how is this magic potion made?
Her face blossomed like a sunflower, and she said—

pour cachaca of your choice, squeeze—a lemon,
mix it with crushed sugar and ice. 'And love?'

She smiled, put a gentle kiss on my cheeks and
said—a great drink must have in it—love distilled.

Candangos

People who built an aeroplane
out of nothing
are remembered fondly
with a sculpture
resembling an alien couple
at the central square of the city.

Candangos are the people who migrated from other parts of Brazil, mainly its Northeast to construct Brasilia.

Carlos Drummond de Andrade

After In the Middle of the Road

In Brazil, there was a poet
there was a poet in Brazil
there was a poet
in Brazil, there was a poet

I will never forget him
in this fleeting life
I will never forget that in Brazil
there was a poet
there was a poet in Brazil
in Brazil, there was a poet.

Carlos Fuentes

The old man rose
from his deathbed
one last time
with good conscience
searching for the place
where air was clear
for humanity
to breathe free
from genocides,
mass murders
and the ever hanging
Damocles' sword
    of war.
Disappointed
he closed his eyes
forever.

Carnival

Prufrock at the Carnival in Rio

Let's go then to Rio, to the Carnival
when drums are beating like heartbeats
of lovers meeting after a long interval
and Samba dancers are out in the streets
Let's go and catch a flight to Rio
Flights full of revelers that take off at night
Oh, do not say no
Let's go

In the Sambadrome dancers come and go
showing off their torso

The colourful floats roll on and on
The colourful marchers sing passionate songs
mesmerized revelers bite their tongues
and shout in drunken madness
swaying back and forth like sea waves
under the full moon February night

There will be time
for the Samba dancers
to move their hips back and forth
there will be time, there will be time
to dance in full glory under the moon
there will be time to steal hearts
moving hands and feet
time for this, time for that
and time yet for a hundred others
before the long night is finally over

In the Sambadrome dancers come and go
showing off their torso

And indeed there will come a moment to ponder
Should I descend the stairs
and join the Samba dancers
with other drunken revelers?
(They will say: what a sport!)
I wear a khaki-colored linen coat, over a white shirt –
linen trousers, the color of dirt
(They will say: how does he dress so smart!)
Should I descend the stairs
and join the carnival?
Eternity hides in a moment
I wait for that moment's arrival

For I have known that such a moment exists
have known that such a moment comes once in ages
and I have waited for it so long
and I know it is coming, it will come
with the music, light and colors of the Carnival
so should I not wait a little more?

And I have seen the world
London, Paris, Amsterdam
New York, Shanghai, Durban
and many other wonders
so where should I end
my journey of years and years
so how should I end?

And I have known other pleasures, known them all
pleasures that belong to grown-up men and women
but Rio Carnival is transcendental, beyond all
Is it the beating of drums
or the bare samba dancers
that make me scream
and then should I assume
this is it?

Shall I say, I have seen all the Samba schools
and watched all the Samba queens

in the Sambadrome, on the top of exotic floats
I should have brought a pair of the best binoculars
to look at these unforgettable, splendid sights

And the night is fully awake filled with joyous screams
People swaying, twirling in *Camarote*
with pouring music, songs beside you and me
Would I after copious drinks and sumptuous dinner
have the strength to leap into the crowd?
But though I have reveled and feasted, reveled and flirted
Though I have seen Samba dancers wearing nothing but paint
riding the floats, performing gymnastic feats
I am no saint – and here is nothing to regret
I have seen this moment of my life etching itself into eternity
and I have seen a drop of water contain an ocean
and I can say it with certainty.

And has it been worth it, after all
After the long wait, crowds, and a night of jostling
among the common men and women in Sambadrome

Has it been worthwhile
to have stood the whole night on my feet
to have left behind my only child
with someone I have hardly known

To say I am Krishna from the *Dwapar* age
I have come to see the *Rasa lila* in Rio

If one, joining the Carnival
should say: the *Rasa lila* is the Carnival of the modern age

And has it been worth it, after all
has it been worth it, after all
after the sea wind that strikes the windowpanes
after the walk over white sands
of Copacabana and Ipanema and so much more

and it is possible to say, this is it
this is it what I meant
it has been worth it after all
to walk over the white sand
to touch sea-waves with one's feet
this is it, this is all

No, I am not Ram or Buddha, nor was meant to be
I am a flirtatious lord, one that will see
a samba queen dance, in her full spree
prod her to do even better
get electric, regal, stately
full of thunderous energy
at times slow and with a pause
but without a dull moment at all

I grow fonder and fonder of the Samba dance
I shall remain forever here in Rio given a chance

Shall I grow my hair and become a *Carioca* cutie?
Shall I go straight to the beach or return to duty?
I have heard Copacabana is full of beauties

I do not think they will look at me
I have seen them lying on the sand
wearing nothing but a book in their hand
lying on the beach between sea and land

We have reveled long in Rio
seen Samba girls in all shades of the rainbow
Shall we go then, shall we return home?

Camarote: Cabin or box in the Sambadrome in Rio de Janeiro
Dwapar: One of the four eons in Hindu mythology
Rasa lila: A dance associated with the story of Krishna, a God in Hindu mythology
Carioca: A permanent resident of the city of Rio de Janeiro

Cartagena

An orange flame
burns in the sky
the city squirms
then revels
inhaling its smell.

Casta

Mestizo, Castizo
Mulatto, Morisco—
sacred flowers blooming
in perfumed gardens
of Latin America.

Castro Alves

Poet, you died
too young

rise
from your grave

the modern slaves
working day and night

need
your songs.

CEASA

Every Saturday Brasilia comes here
putting all its scandals and worries to rest

a sea of fruits, vegetables, flowers, coffee,
cheese, meat, everyone picks one's best

sweet sounds of people talking, aroma
there is nothing here that I detest

where do I go from here, I'm drunk
my restless eyes lost in this beauty fest.

CEASA: A Saturday market for vegetables, fruit etc. in Brasilia.

Cecilia Meireles

'The afternoon wind comes and goes between India and Brazil tirelessly.'
– Cecilia Meireles

India in my heart
and mind, I set out
on the high seas
sailing with the wind,
Gandhi and Tagore
long gone, but
I hope to see Nehru
and India's glorious cities—
Delhi, Calcutta, Hyderabad, Bombay,
the ghats of the holy Ganges
in Patna and Benares
and for a while the streams
of the Amazon and the Ganges
unite and flow together,
Rio and Calcutta speak
to each other, Sao Paulo
and Bombay samba together,
the cows of Brazil return
home to meet their long lost cousins
and the afternoon wind comes and goes
between India and Brazil tirelessly.

Ghats: Banks

César Vallejo

After Mass

The corpse
who was already dead
died again this Thursday
in Paris
all men, women, and children
on the earth
could not save him
from dying again,
he wished to get up slowly
at least once
to embrace the last human
before dying again.

Chasquis

Time changes everything.
The skilled, agile runners
who kept the Inca empire running
carrying *quipu* – talking knots in one hand
and *pututu* – conch shells in another
balancing themselves on rope bridges
over gorges and valleys
transporting presents on their backs
running over two hundred miles a day,
now rest at the Larco Museum
with a long nose like Pinnochio
wearing a sun shaped crown
and a garland, all made of gold.

Che Guevara

'Man truly achieves his full human condition when he produces without being compelled by the physical necessity of selling himself as a commodity.' – Che Guevara

If we met and sat together
we would recite Kipling's 'If',
read Neruda, Lorca, Whitman
travel across Latin America

on the way to Machu Picchu
we would see the same
exquisite beauty and crushing poverty
that you saw riding your motorcycle

we would write the same poem,
though I would not kill
I would forgive them as Gandhi did
I would wield a pen, not a gun.

Chico Mendes

'At first I thought I was fighting to save rubber trees, then I thought I was fighting to save the Amazon rainforest. Now I realize I am fighting for humanity.' – Chico Mendes

The assassin's bullets killed me
I stopped breathing
to give the breath of the world

a new lease of life,
my dreams became the dreams
of humanity to save itself from itself

a thousand Chico Mendes reincarnated
across the planet to face the bullets
of a thousand assassins.

Christ the Redeemer

A gigantic white angel
stands on the mountain Corcovado
looking at the Guanabara Bay
white sands of Ipanema shines in his eyes

in the evening his shadow falls
over favelas, as night falls
and the city sleeps,
he takes off the mountain

swoops over the city
admiring its exquisite beauty
trying to redeem it
of its sins, but helpless

he returns every dawn
to the mountain
and turns into a statue,
his hands spread, wings folded

to keep his legend alive
to make people believe in his power
who visit him in hordes every day
braving tropical heat and vertigo.

Clarice Lispector

'The terrible duty is to go to the end.' – Clarice Lispector

Clarice comes in my dreams
walking on water

her body light
as an autumn leaf in mid-air

I ask her about her mother
she utters very slowly—pogroms

I ask her about her father
she says—a botched operation

I ask her about her sisters
she says—their husbands

I ask her about her husband
she looks at her sons and says nothing

I wake up
smothered by her silence.

Cuba

I often tell myself this—
someday I'll learn Spanish
and travel to Cuba
to learn how to roll a Cuban Cigar
and pose smoking
    in Havana
will bask under the sun at sandy Varadero,
watch a million crabs cross the road
    on their way to the Bay of Pigs,
will dive in cenotes and drink
    some rum or daiquiri
and dance salsa in the underground
someday,
I often tell myself this.

Cusco

Cobblestoned streets
still carry traces of the Incas

evening murmur of tourists
just back from Machu Picchu

silent, hushed, cold nights
warmed with pisco sour and coca tea

An old lady with her llama
wearing her traditional Andean dress

—red hat, multi-colored shawl
embroidered jacket, black skirt

tries to cross the street—
her mouth open, eyes lost in trance.

Day of the Dead

'Todos somos calaveras.' – Jose Guadalupe Posada

'We are all skeletons'
on the day of the dead

fierce pumas in red
move with feline grace

back to the Earth
in the realm of the living,

tread softly on the bed
of marigold flowers

smelling copal incense smoke,
skull-skeletons taste sweet bread

and make fun of the living
with their literary calaveras.

Copal: Aromatic resins from copal tree used by pre-Columbian cultures

E

Eduardo Galeano

A Letter to Eduardo Galeano

Dear Eduardo,

The open veins of Latin America
have been cut open wider
since your departure,
new veins are being cut open every day,
the number of workers in the vein opening industry
has multiplied,
unemployment rate has significantly dropped,
inflation has also come down,
isn't it development? What else would you call development?
There are new vampires on the horizon with globalization,
their hunger for blood and wealth has exponentially grown
Amazon has many veins. Amazon is burning.
It will open many veins instantaneously.

Hope you're well and not turning in your grave.
Please do not. There is hardly anyone left who can fix
damaged graves these days.
Everyone is employed in the vein opening industry.
Therefore, please rest in peace.

Yours sincerely,
The Poet

El Ateneo

Tango dancers
    turn into books,
        dazzle as diamonds
            in the grand golden
                crown of the city.

F

Favelas

Party-coloured
    islands
in the sea
    of an indifferent
humanity
    suffering,
        celebrating
the carnival
    i.e. life.

Formosa

The moon waited
for me with its sickle
in the east

having reaped
stars from the cosmic
harvest field

while I traveled at night
drunk on life's nectar
from Formosa to Brasilia.

Frida Kahlo

'I joyfully await the exit—and I hope never to return.'
– Frida Kahlo

A paralyzed hummingbird
wearing a necklace of thorns
her tiny fluttering wings
painting the canvas

a crashed wooden bus
scattered bones
blood and water
a green frog swims in it

its eyes large and red
a blue house on its tongue
lovers hover around—
summer flies

a lady wrapped in yellow
butterflies in Manhattan
at the peak
of the Great Depression

a malevolent Paris
an empty Louvre
with just one painting—
pink and white

an elephant trumpets alone
a flying bed, a silent
Frida lies where
a beam of light leaps out.

G

Gabriel Garcia Marquez

For a hundred years
    I have been
walking on water
    looking
at the golden fish
    leaping out
in the air
    butterflies
racing past
    trains
full of gypsies
    recounting
bizarre tales.

Gabriela Mistral

After Dame la Mano

Read me your poem and we shall float
freely across the cosmos like a comet,
read me your poem and I'll be blessed
like a butterfly drunk on nectar

We shall drink the same verse
from the fountain of the universe
like two hummingbirds in mid-air,
like two hummingbirds, nothing more

You're swift wind, and I am a fearless horse
and we shall leap together to the moon
because we are two bodies
but one soul and nothing more.

Honduras

'*Gracias a Dios que hemos salido de esas Honduras.*'
– Christopher Columbus

Thank God
we have departed from those depths
and after this final voyage
we can rest.

I

Iguazu Falls

Birds have taken over the sky
a butterfly lands on my hand

vapour rises high
instantly turning into clouds

I am silent, letting
the moment seep in

a quatis comes close
with her sad eyes

I walk on the paved trail
dumbfounded, drenched

as nature mourns
for our dying planet

I stand in silence
listening to Iguazu falls

watching a thousand rainbows
rise in the sky

I walk to the devil's throat
I am in the lap of eternity

I try to see her face—
it's blinding white.

Inhotim

Imagination at its edge —
a phantasma larger than life
at every step
    springing a surprise.

Inhotim is home to one of the largest foundations of contemporary art near Belo Horizonte near Brazil and is one of the largest outdoor art centers in Latin America.

Isla Negra

i

Abundant as the sea
a poet should live like this

the sun rising above one's head
and setting at one's feet

surrounded by memories
of childhood

harnessing sea waves
channelizing them into creativity

a dozen suits, a hundred ties
thousands of seashells, butterflies

a horse with three tails
Nataraja above the fireplace

ii

Sea waves of the Pacific,
do you know, a poet

lives here surrounded
by his toys, books,

large wooden statues,
animal heads, wines

of a thousand kinds,
the captain's boat

grounded on the sand
he sails it

with his friends
over a drink or two—

a wooden horse from Temuco
a woolen sheep by the bedside

the sound of falling rain
on the tin roof—

the poet travels back and forth
in time between his birthplace

and the world, seeking
refuge in his childhood.

Itamaraty

Anaesthetized, clinical, green
ready to build the scalpel
of words—to slash, to heal.

Itiquira Falls

A water cathedral
falls—
vapor angels rise.

J

Jaguar

Web search shows
I'm a car brand

my rosettes missing
from the internet

my piercing eyes
printed on the third page.

Jorge Amado

I saw the captains of sands
in Salvador, Bahia of all the Saints,

kicking footballs
on the Porto da Barra beach

I asked them if they knew
Jorge Amado, the writer

– they asked me – 'Jorge who?'
I said loudly – Jorge Amado

they looked at the football
and kicked it hard,

it fell in Amado's house
there I found an old typewriter

which bore his fingerprints,
his colourful shirts

smelling of sea, women,
cinnamon and cloves—

on the wall
Marx, Lenin, Ganesha

a Maithuna couple
dancing to the sound

of Condomble rituals,
books waiting to be opened.

Condomble is an Afro-Brazilian religious tradition practiced in Salvador, Bahia, Brazil.

Julio Cortazar

"Literature is a game, but it's a game one can put one's life into."
– Julio Cortazar

'What is Literature?'
—I asked Cortazar

He didn't answer.
Hence this game

of words—to find
order in chaos.

King Penguins

Bright orange cheek patch
like the sun setting below the horizon

against surrounding dark feathers
like the black of the night

Nearly wiped out
by man—

the natives of the Tierra del Fuego
have returned home.

L

La Chascona

Wearing stars in her feet
she points towards

the entangled galaxy
—Neruda's secret home

and whispers gently
—love happens.

La Recoleta

Death asks life at La Recoleta
how long will you last ?

Look at me, I'm eternal—
the final truth.

Come, rest amidst these exquisite stones,
give in, the universe is my necropolis.

La Sebastiana

A cat prowls in Neruda's house
I'm lost—
    one moment I look at her,
another at the remains of the poet.

Lima

When the last sun rays fall on colonial facades,
the Inca temples and pre-Columbian ruins
along the Costa Verde,
I climb the crumbling cliffs
then descend down the Malecon
to surf the waves of the Pacific

listen to solemn chants of Peru
and its sublime poetry,
get submerged
in its history and meet
Chimú, Chancay, Chincha,
Nazca and Inca at the Museo Larco

cross the bridge of sighs in Barranco
and go to crowded nightclubs
to dance to the tropical beats,
when I'm tired,
find my way
through Lima's messy streets

or go to Puruchuco
all tied up in ropes—head to toe
and lie with a mummy
and then to Pachacamac
to climb the pyramids
to bow to the Earth Maker

head to the Love Park
to smell the rose blooming in the desert
and look at the Lima Bay,
climb the Huaca Pucllana,
taste Chicha Morada
and pisco sour by the river Rimac

enter the abode of last Inca on the San Cristobal Hill
get inside Lima's old train station—a time machine
and see it metamorphose into an extraordinary thing,
look at intricately carved wooden balconies
at the Plaza de Armas and steal a glimpse
of the Gran Hotel Bolivar at San Martin

watch the masked dancers dancing Chonguinada
and pigeons hovering over the San Francisco Cathedral—
the flying spirits of those buried underneath the labyrinth
of catacombs, and then go to Larcomar
to watch the sun set over the Pacific, and to top it all
let my spirit soar with a thousand fountains at the aqua park.

Abhay K.

Lorca and I in New York

I feel happy here
the sky is gloomy, it's freezing
outside, high-rise concrete buildings
not a single tree around
I am warm
    lying in room 1512
at the Park Central
    I feel at home
New York's cold yellowish bricks
feel warm, pedestrians appear
Whitmanesque strangers
I smile
    and want them
to smile back

Trees in Central Park
have shed their leaves
and a flock of black-birds
sit over them
    forming canopies,
the sun is not back yet
from the new year holidays
yet I feel warm

I see a shadow—an apparition
it must be Lorca, I feel intuitively,
who walked once in these streets.
I follow him—his duende—towards
Columbia University, he takes
unexpected turns, I keep
following him
he stops and asks me
to walk with him across
Brooklyn Bridge, we look

at the river, still not frozen,
and head towards the United Nations

I am curious what Lorca would say
at the UNGA rostrum
he stands firm, and I lend him my ears
I can't make out what he says—
it's pure poetry, not a politician's speech
Lorca speaks in figures, not words
I clap alone, nobody else is here

We walk out looking at the knotted gun
and laugh, in lower Manhattan
at Poets House we hear
contemporary Poets
Lorca whispers in my ears—
"where is poetry...
is it lost in prose or in rap
or in soulful lyrics
of the Tambourine man
in the great American song tradition?"

We decide to go
to Broadway
to watch a play
we leave it in the middle
and get into a yellow taxi—
the driver Mandip tells us
how he came
from Jalandhar to New York
seventeen years ago and never
returned to India fearing
arranged marriage
but his worst fears came true

Lorca himself had been through this
before he left the shores of Spain

for New York to forget his bitter love
He whispered in my ears—
'I might have tried
arranged-marriage myself
had they not killed me in cold blood.'

Lucio Costa

The original lord of geometry
fiddling with triangles,
squares, bows and arrows
giving wings to the dream
and the prophecy of Brasilia.

M

Machado de Assis

What is life—love, lust, misery, death
—floating islands of happiness
in a sea of despair?

Can one leave this world
a little happier, a little less
miserable, and win the life's race?

Perhaps, there's an answer,
buried in the grave
of Bras Cubas?

Machu Picchu

What do the dancing stones
of Machu Picchu tell us—

when earthquakes or storms
threaten to turn us into dust

—dance and celebrate
no matter what comes our way,

those who dance, endure and stay
those who don't, are blown away.

Machu Picchu Train

Two baby donkeys look
innocently at the train

moving back and forth
on the zigzag path

farmers harvesting corn, smile
waving at the passing train

dogs run along the track, barking
the train chugs through the valley

mountain cows amble lazily and graze
in the countryside covered in morning haze

blue sky enters the wagon
through the transparent ceiling

Andean flute plays, the train passes
occasionally through small towns

and the curious children peep out
of windows of the old houses.

Manaus

Where rivers meet
bearing different colours

and an opera is heard
in the middle of the jungle

there I meet my other self
on banks of the Amazon.

Mario Vargas Llosa

'I believe that the great danger in our age is nationalism, it's no longer fascism, nor communism.' – Mario Vargas Llosa

He lives with a pen in his hand
having come out of the tribe
of nations—
    he is now a world citizen.

Medellin

They walk in the streets of El Poblado
hanging out in cafes and bars
eating salads, drinking lemonades

stopping and posing
in front of the sculptures
of voluptuous women and men

they keep walking, asking
directions for nowhere, getting lost
finding each other again and again

drinking lemonade and coconut water
street vendors keep coming, trying
aggressively to sell them aphrodisiacal ants

they laugh out loud and learn
what it means to be happy
to live every moment

they read poems on cities, hop
in a taxi and nearly get killed
with rash driving in Medellin

they listen to poets and singers
looking at their funny portraits
haggling over the price of popcorn

sit side by side on the floor lighting
candles, looking at the waxing moon,
reciting Hafez— "the sun never says

to Earth—'you owe me', look
what happens with love like that,
it lights up the whole sky,"

and they see light, they dance slowly
at night looking at the shooting stars
and they see a balloon man taking off

the ground and people murmuring
in disbelief about such supernatural
things happening in Medellin.

Moai

What are you
waiting for Moai?

Your eyes always open
without blinking

what's so urgent
in this world,

whose arrival
do you await?

If you are looking
for a saviour

there is none,
no one will come

this far to save you
even by chance

you're on your own
we're all on our own

close your eyes,
go home and sleep.

Moon Valley

There is nothing
like moon here

large sand dunes
and scattered rocks

rechristened as Tres Marias,
a *Mirante* to watch the sunset

Magic sets in with the last sun rays
falling on the mountains

and volcanic craters, turning
it into a Martian landscape.

Mirante: A high point to look at the valley.

Moon Rising Over Brasilia

Moon rising over Brasilia—
a longing rising in my heart

to see it and you
without blinking

to follow moon
and your body

through the night
until it sets and you rise.

Nazca Lines

Mysterious lines
reveal the sacred

geometry of the heavens—condor,
monkey, spider, whale, hummingbird

each on their own journey
through the universe.

Neruda

What did my father say
when I showed him
my first poem

what did the pariah Tamil girl say
whom I thought to be
a thousand-year old goddess

I raped her thinking
it—'the coming together
of a man and a statue'

what did my ailing daughter say
before she died aged eight
in Nazi-occupied Netherlands

did I hear her voice
coming
    from across the ocean

what did the dissident poets say
in freezing Siberian gulags listening
to my ode to the Kremlin highlander

what did the doctor say
before injecting me in the stomach
at a Santiago hospital

I died six and a half hours later.
Now I've been exhumed
I am trying to remember.

Nicaragua

After Gioconda Belli

Nicaragua!
What are you—

sacred water of a powerful chieftain
of an Amerindian tribe

or a white tree in the lake Nicaragua
covered with herons

words of Ruben Dario,
Ernesto Cardenal or Gioconda Belli

or hum of a rare hummingbird
drinking nectar from fragrant flowers

are you the song of revolution
or sound of the bell of La Merced

the drab of a dynasty
or hope for the downtrodden

are you a hellfire ready to erupt
just like your active volcanoes?

Nicanor Parra

'*Me retracto de todo lo dicho*' – Nicanor Parra

Take back
    I take back
        everything
    everything I have said
        I take back
Take back

O

Octavio Paz

'History is one thing, our lives something else...I have survived, that's enough...'
– Octavio Paz

Staring at a draft of shadows
I straddle between two pasts

my feet on two boats
I keep afloat composing poems

I am alone in a library
reading forbidden books

I lose my faith reading Voltaire
the library crumbles in front of my eyes

I am happy
I have survived

I come across godemiches in Paris
don't know what are these

embarrassed, I ask a surrealist,
who whispers in my ears—

'these are objects to overcome
profound human loneliness.'

I think all fighting is absurd
but cannot tell it to anyone

so I go to see Neruda
he calls me a traitor

then embraces me affectionately
calling me—'son.'

Meeting Buddha in India
on the footpath, I ask—

'what is Self?' Buddha smiles
and turns into a pile of stones.

Oscar Niemeyer

The lord of geometry
the lover of sensuous curves
a seer from the future—
lord Vishwakarma's
Brazilian avatar.

Lord Vishwakarma: Presiding Hindu deity of architects, engineers

Oswald de Andrade

'Tupi or not Tupi, that is the question.'
– Oswald de Andrade, *Cannibal Manifesto*

We are all cannibals—
when we colonizers landed
in the new world,
we cannibalized the Tupi
accusing the Tupi
of practicing cannibalism.

Ouro Preto

Hidden in the mountains,
it appears suddenly like a fairy-land

its sky pierced with domes, cupolas,
turrets, time stands still

its streets cobblestoned
exactly as in the eighteenth century

at the peak of the Gold Rush
when more people walked

in these streets than in New York
its churches overflowing with gold

flea markets full of soapstone statues
except of Tiradentes, who was hanged

at the city square for conspiring
to overthrow the Portuguese empire.

P

Panama Canal

A dense jungle
infested with venomous snakes

insects, spiders—yellow fever, malaria
the death toll—two hundred per month

twenty-two thousand dead
within eight years of digging

project abandoned
changed hands

diplomatic upheavals
birth of a new country*

and silver and gold rolls
still unmixed, segregated

float in the canal water
telling tales of humanity's dark days.

* It was the first time in history that a canal created a new county.

The gold roll and the silver roll were racially coded payroll categories of workers employed by the U.S. builders of the Panama Canal.

Papal Bull

A papal bull is not a bull
but it walks in public squares

with or without a pope
with its two heads

looking left and right
through its leaden seal.

Paramaribo

Alonso, Juan, Amerigo—
the voyagers rushed

to the Wild Coast
in search of an Inca El Dorado

instead they discovered Parmurbo—
a village inhabited by the Indians

and when the tobacco and sugar
plantations declined

a mighty city arose
on the banks of the river Suriname.

Now, Wilhelmina—
the displaced Dutch queen

looks at Goslar—a sunken ghost ship
from a rusty island.

Paraty

A heron sits by a lagoon
on the rocks covered with moss

a lonely grey horse grazes
occasionally disturbed by dogs

little birds are busy in the grass
chirping, hopping with joy

clouds descend on green hills
morning joggers pass by

sea waves make splashing sounds
distant islands shine

under the groves, the young
do their morning yoga

listening to Sanskrit chants
I walk slowly on the beach

taking a deep breath, wishing
every dawn on Earth be like it.

ii

A loving sea enters
the city every day
on some pretext or the other.

iii

Leandro on his horse carriage
gives me a city tour—

it is the house of Amir Klinky
—the writer from Paraty

here is the central square
—Praca de Matriz

this is a cemetery
that's a church built in 1880.

iv

Paraty is a cock's
kookrookoo at five thirty

Bruno's zen yoga
from six to seven

Diego's restless hands at noon
photographing everything

Evelyn's dentured smile
in the evening.

Perito Moreno

Blocks of blue
ice floats on water

trapping a handful of sky
and poison

of the blue-throated god
Shiva.

Perito Moreno is a glacier in Argentina
Shiva is a Hindu God

Peru

I have had dreams of Peru
ever since I was born—

a magical world of mountains
and valleys full of butterflies

dry salt pans and circular farms
lofty peaks kissing the sun

sacred waters of the Ganges
mixing with waters of the Urubamba

and *Mandar Parvat* hidden in the Andes
from the prying eyes of *Devas* and *Asuras*

after the great churning of the ocean
sparing Shiva of another bout of *halahala*

I have seen myself flying over
the sacred valley and the Inca ruins

lying with mummies
tightly wrapped from head to toe

metamorphosing into monkey, spider,
hummingbird, condor or flamingo.

Devas and Asuras: Gods and demons
Mandar Parvat: A mountain used as a churning rod
Halahala: Poison that came out of churning of the sea

Porto Alegre

Those who live
in Brasilia
I tell them to go
to Porto Alegre

to take a dip
in the river Guaiba
to drink beauty
at *Padre Chagasa*

what is left in a city
    white as death
Porto Alegre has all
    a young heart craves.

Padre Chagasa is a posh street in Porto Alegre.

Q

Quetzal

Resplendent god of the air
wearing iridescent green feathers
bring us light,
freedom, wealth and spring.

Quetzalcoatl

'He was the wind; he was the guide, the road sweeper of the rain gods, of the masters of the water, of those who brought rain.'
—Anales del Museo Nacional de México

Snake god, harbinger of rain,
wind and wisdom
wearing breastplate, shell jewelry,
conical hat, ear-rings of jade circles,
spiral shells, conch whorl, red mask
like a duck's bill, flanked by quetzals—
feathered serpent, bless the earth.

R

Roque Dalton

After Poema del Amor

Candangos who built Brasilia
are remembered by a sculpture
at the *Praça dos Três Poderes*
resembling an alien couple

slaves who were brought
from Africa to plow the fields
of Latin America, and who
continue to inhabit the favelas

countless indigenous tribes
and nations who were exterminated
by disease, slavery, murder
after the invasion of the colonizers

for all those nameless who perished
at the hands of military juntas
and during wars and revolutions—
here is a love poem for you all.

Ruben Dario

After Lo Fatal

Man is happy for he is alive
like a Quetzal full of colours—flying
no greater joy than to live and thrive
no deeper despair than dying

to be, to know, to find one's way
the bliss of having lived and to hope
that tomorrow will be better than today
why worry about what we don't know

to live every moment, laugh, travel
to indulge in the pleasures of flesh, revel
for death is certain for everyone who is born
from void we emerge, to void we return.

S

Salvador, Bahia

Cobblestoned pathways of Pelourinho
multi-coloured houses

I walk here for days and nights
travel back in time

and sit at the stairs of Praca de Pelourinho
listening to cries of slaves being whipped, wrenched

looking at the cascading silhouettes
of houses lined up to Carmo

I go up and down using the Lacerda
my eyes filled with light

of the sun rising and setting at the All Saints Bay
then sit silently sharing solitude of fort Mont Serrat

moon peeps at me through palm leaves
sing in unison with the boisterous crowd at Bomfim

I tie around my wrist coloured wish-ribbons
walk on water in the dike of Tororo

with the Candomble gods and goddesses
travel back and forth in time

with Castro Alves and Jorge Amado
turn into whale fat and burn

lighting up Farol de Baha, speak Tupi-Guarani
bring the Amerindians back to life

grant freedom to slaves, restore lost tribes
transform favelas of Bonoco and Periperi

into securely gated condominiums by magic
while people wait for their Salvador.

Samba

A beam of light
enters a dark alley—
spirit takes over body.

San Cristobal

She sees all
hears all—
says nothing.

San Pedro de Atacama

A laughter at night
pierces vast sadness
of the Atacama.

San Salvador

Amidst abandoned ruins of the Nahuatl nation
a city lies at the coast of the Pacific ocean
between a lake and a volcano

under a blue and yellow dome
rests archbishop Oscar A. Romero
and the Plaza Gerardo Barrios remembers

that historic day the Chapultepec accords
were signed ending the civil war
and scores of people had flooded the city square.

* Chapultepec accords in 1992 ended a decade of Civil War in El Salvador.

Santiago Snippets

i

guarded by the Andes
wearing a veil of smoke
—Santiago

ii

lovers in different poses
rest in the park—
sculptures frozen in time

iii

water flows
from Simon Bolivar's mouth
— a tree laden with crows

iv

La Moneda—
journey of centuries
from back to front

v

a set of locks
adorn puente Pio Nono—
a dry river below

vi

shops, shops, and shops
at Patio Bellavista—
plenty to eat

vii

a sea of shops
at Parque Arauco—
nothing to nibble

viii

a castle
a green toy train—
the stuff of the fairies

ix

the last sun rays of April
set fire to the Andes—
amber peaks

x

to Piedra Rosa
chauffeur Jorge loses his way
—full moon.

São Paulo

Giant towers rise
in concrete jungles

birds are absent from the sky
trees pray for sunlight.

Simon Bolivar

all who served the revolution
have plowed the sea—
these were the last words
of the man who fought
472 battles and rode twice
on horseback as much as
Alexander the Great
to liberate Latin America
from the Spanish rule

he kept his solemn vow
not to marry again
after the untimely death
of his young wife Maria
though had countless affairs.

Tango Girl from Caminito, La Boca

She wears a red dress
her eyes smile
looking at the strangers

she invites them to tango
a shy young man comes forward
she puts a hat on his head

asks him to look into her eyes
and bends backward
letting him hold her

her left leg stretched
her right arm raised
pushing his left palm

towards the sky
her right leg rests
on his slightly bent left knee

they freeze
like a sculpture
for a fleeting moment.

Tarsila do Amaral

A giant negra
with only one breast
devouring Europe

a huge footed maneater
sitting by a trident cactus
devouring the golden sun.

Tikal

The temple of voices rises in the air
like the Mahabodhi temple

a Mayan Buddha meditates
under the giant Kapok tree.

Tijuca Forest

My eyes, still drunk with beauty
of the goddess of Tijuca forest

she wears a crown of flowers
birds, butterflies hover around her

she walks through the forest
the devil warns—time is up—

blows thc horn, she keeps walking —
keeps singing—tu ta tu tu ta—

tu ta tu tu ta, the devil vanishes
at the Chinese point—she sees

a thousand hills rising out of the sea
and jumps shouting wooooohooooo!

Toucan

From where did you get your colourful bill
sharp, shining as a fashionista's heel

what an exquisite sexual ornament
— thought Charles Darwin!

Tenochtitlan

One day when I woke up
I saw Mexico city
had turned into Tenochtitlan

It must be a dream—I thought
and scratched myself
to be sure I was not asleep—

clocks had not turned back—
the mankind had corrected its follies, and
the world had become pure and pristine.

U

Ushuaia

Even at the end of the world
there is no dearth of light

periphery becomes the center
and the centre—the periphery

there I float in silence
at the feet of the snow-covered hills.

Uyuni Salt Planes

Giant mirrors
reveal—
the universe's face.

V

Valparaiso

Sea is dull
streets stale
reeking of decay
ageing and death

colours play
hide and seek
in a floating cloud
of mist at Neruda's house

I see a nymph—
it hurts to look at her
and hurts even more
to look away—

is she the one
whom Neruda saw
from his window
every Sunday?

Victoria Ocampo

An ailing poet sheltered
in her home, her heart

she—his *Vijaya*
— his poetry, his life—

Victoria and Tagore—
two souls dancing in ecstasy

Purabi blowing incessantly
between India and Argentina.

Vijaya: Victoria
Purabi: Easterly wind

W

West Indies

With deep quest to find India
Columbus sailed in his ships

and stumbled into the islands
where no Indians ever lived

he still insisted to call them Indians
and the islands—the West Indies!

Is this how and where the story
of Latin America begin?

X

Xnipec

I eat it till I cry—
my nose wet,
stomach burning

I wander around
Yucatan through the night
seeking remedies.

Xnipec is a very hot salsa of Yucantan peninsula in Mexico.

Xunantunich

The stone woman's
ghost wanders at night
dressed in white

her eyes glowing red
hot lava
erupting from a volcano

she climbs the stairs
and disappears
in the stone wall.

Xunantunich is an ancient Maya archaeological site in Belize.

Y

Yemanja

The Yoruba goddess
emerges out of water

the city walks to her
in joyous rapture

her body covered
with offerings—

pure white roses,
corn-meal, water-melons

the creator goddess,
protector of seamen

gives her blessings to all
with cowrie shells in her hands.

Z

Zocalo

In the middle of this vast square
I stand alone, meditating—
racing back and forth in time

hearing jeers of the victors
silence of the vanquished
all swept away by time's broom

does it matter who loses, who wins a war—
a people, a tribe, a nation is destroyed
only to reincarnate in another form.

Acknowledgements

I would like to thank Kirk Greenway, Indran Amirthanayagam and Chaitali Pandya for going carefully through the book and making valuable suggestions. I am grateful to Forrest Gander, Ruth Padel, Víctor Rodríguez Núñez, Gabriel Rosenstock, Zoe Brigley Thompson, Nicholas Birns, Mauricio Santaro, Ambassador Jorge Heine and Ambassador R. Vishwanathan for their valuable comments about the book.

Some poems included in this collection have appeared earlier: 'Borges,' 'Prufrock at the Carnival in Rio,' and 'César Vallejo' in *Poetry Salzburg Review* (Salzburg, Austria, issue 30, autumn 2016); 'Belmopan,' 'Brasilia,' 'Lima,' 'Paramaribo,' and 'San Salvador' in *CAPITALS* (Bloomsbury India, 2017); 'Candangos,' 'Castro Alves,' 'CEASA,' Formosa,' 'Moon rising over Brasilia,' and 'Oscar Niemeyer' in *The Prophecy of Brasilia* (Colletivo Editorial, 2018, Brazil); 'Neruda' in *Madras Courier* (2019); 'I and Lorca in New York' in *Buenos Aires Poetry* (2019) in Spanish translation; 'Neruda' in *Descontexto* (2018) in Spanish translation; 'Octavio Paz,' 'Frida Kahlo,' and 'Carlos Fuentes' in *Blanco Movil* (Mexico, 2019) in Spanish translation.